KU-477-800

Made with Love

How Babies Are Made

Illustrated by

Charlotte Middleton

Written by

Kate Petty

MACMILLAN
CHILDREN'S BOOKS

"You grew in my tummy. Everyone in the world was once a baby in their mum's tummy."

"A sperm from your dad joined up with an egg inside me."

A woman is born with eggs inside her.
A man has sperm.

An egg is smaller than a single grain of sand.
Sperm are much, much smaller than eggs.

"So dads have sperm..."

"And mums have eggs!"

"It happened when your dad and I made love."

When a dad and a mum love each other and want to make a baby, they make love. This is also called having sex.

A mum has a vagina and a dad has a penis.

penis

vagina

The dad and the mum hold each other close so the dad's penis can fit into the mum's vagina. The sperm come out of the penis into the vagina.

"The sperm swam like tadpoles to the egg."

Millions of sperm race to where the egg
is waiting, but only one sperm gets
to join up with the egg.
This is called "fertilisation".
Sometimes none of the sperm joins up
with the egg, so a baby can't be made.

egg

sperm

"I wonder if we've made a baby?"

"I hope so."

"As soon as they joined together, the egg began to grow and change into you."

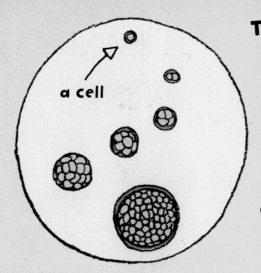

a cell

The fertilised egg starts off as a tiny dot called a "cell". This cell divides into two cells. Then those cells divide again and again until there are millions of cells.

This ball of cells travels to the mum's womb, which is a special place inside her tummy. Inside the mum's womb, the baby floats in a liquid to keep it safe.

"This is where I grew."

"When did I start to look like a baby?"

"Well, at first you looked more like a little fish than a baby. You even had a tail."

embryo

After about four weeks, the ball of cells had turned into a tiny "embryo", about the size of a pea.

(larger than life size)

This then turned into a baby-shaped "foetus", which grew like this.

Actual size at 10 weeks

at 3 months

at 6 months

"Yes, you stayed there for nine months, and as you grew my tummy got bigger and bigger."

"Could you feel me moving inside you?"

"Yes, I could feel you stretching and kicking."

The baby practises moving. At first it feels like a butterfly fluttering its wings. As the baby gets bigger, the mum feels it turning and squirming.

Sometimes you can even see a big baby move — it makes the mum's tummy move.

"I can feel the baby moving!"

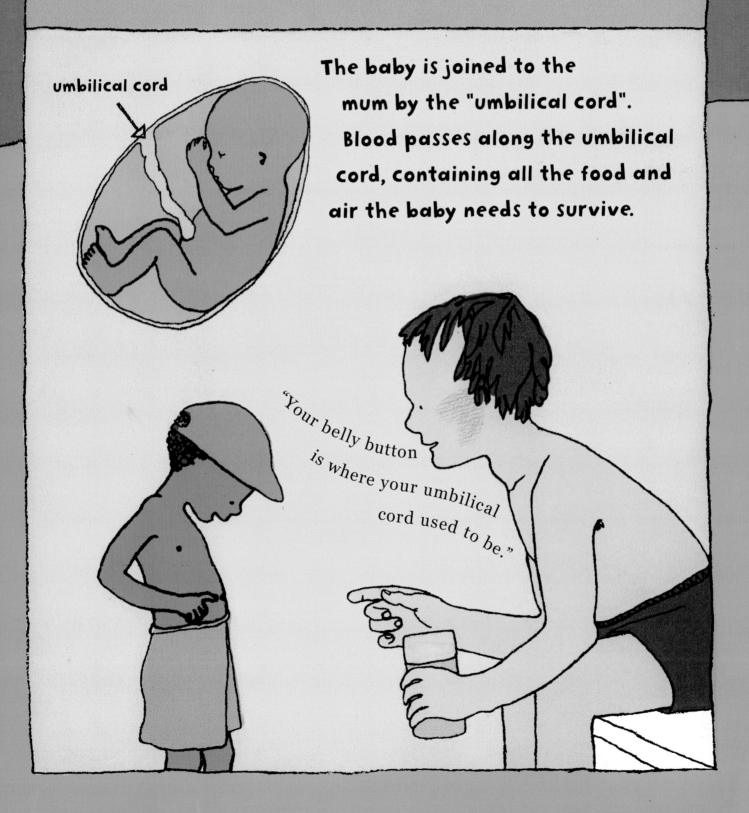

"How did you know when I was ready to be born?"

"The muscles in my body began to push you out."

"Nearly there!"

After nine months a baby is ready to be born.
The mum's muscles work hard to push the baby out
of her womb. Babies usually come out head first.

"What was the first thing I did
when I was born?"